MY BO

MY BODY H

NOSE

AMY CULLIFORD

A Crabtree Roots Plus Book

CRABTREE
Publishing Company
www.crabtreebooks.com

School-to-Home Support for Caregivers and Teachers

This book helps children grow by letting them practice reading. Here are a few guiding questions to help the reader with building his or her comprehension skills. Possible answers appear here in red.

Before Reading:

- What do I think this book is about?
  - *I think this book is about my nose.*
  - *I think this book is about how my nose smells things.*
- What do I want to learn about this topic?
  - *I want to learn about why my nostrils have hair inside.*
  - *I want to learn why I sneeze through my nose.*

During Reading:

- I wonder why...
  - *I wonder why my nose sometimes gets stuffy.*
  - *I wonder why I only have two nostrils.*
- What have I learned so far?
  - *I have learned that my nose helps me smell things.*
  - *I have learned that my nose helps me breathe air.*

After Reading:

- What details did I learn about this topic?
  - *I have learned that people breathe fast when they run and slow when they sleep.*
  - *I have learned that there are different kinds of smells.*
- Read the book again and look for the vocabulary words.
  - *I see the word **nostrils** on page 8 and the word **stuffy** on page 16. The other vocabulary words are found on page 23.*

You have a **nose**.

It is between your eyes.

It is part of your face.

Noses can be big
or small.

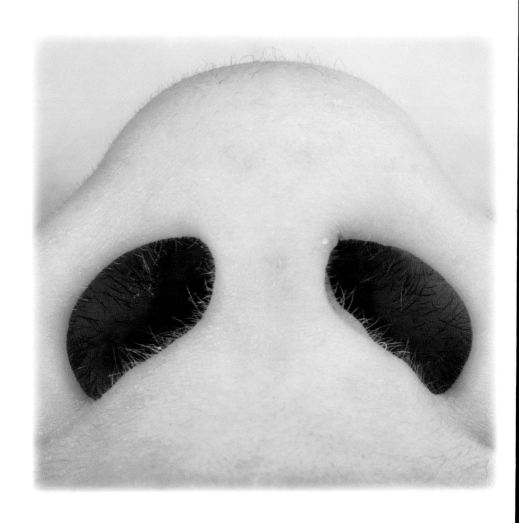

Your nose has
two **nostrils**.

They help you take in
and let out air.

Your nose helps
you **breathe**!

Sometimes we breathe fast.

Sometimes we breathe slow.

Some things make our nose **sneeze**.

Our nose can also get **stuffy**. Sophia has a cold.

Your nose helps you **smell** things.

Some things smell bad.

Some things smell good!

Word List
Sight Words

a	has	small
air	have	some
also	help	sometimes
and	helps	take
bad	in	they
be	is	things
between	it	two
big	let	we
can	make	you
cold	of	your
eyes	or	
face	our	
fast	out	
get	part	
good	slow	

Words to Know

breathe

nose

nostrils

smell

sneeze

stuffy

MY BODY
MY BODY HAS A
NOSE

Written by: Amy Culliford

Designed by: Rhea Wallace

Series Development: James Earley

Proofreader: Janine Deschenes

Educational Consultant: Marie Lemke M.Ed.

Print and production coordinator:

Katherine Berti

Photographs:
Shutterstock: Groundback Ateller: cover, p. 1; Ty Lim: p. 3; Yulia Cherry: p. 4; Rido: p. 5; Miramiska: p. 7; Deyan Georglev: p. 8; Fizkes: p. 9; Yuliya Eustrateriko; Anurak Pongpatiment: p. 12; Vadym Postukh: p. 13; Gundam_AI; p. 15; Prostock_studio: p. 16; sirtravelalot: p. 17; pictor picture: p. 19

Library and Archives Canada Cataloguing in Publication

Available at the Library and Archives Canada

Library of Congress Cataloging-in-Publication Data

Available at the Library of Congress

Crabtree Publishing Company

www.crabtreebooks.com   1-800-387-7650

Printed in the U.S.A./CG20210915/012022

Published in the United States
Crabtree Publishing
347 Fifth Avenue, Suite 1402-145
New York, NY, 10016

Published in Canada
Crabtree Publishing
616 Welland Ave.
St. Catharines, Ontario L2M 5V6